HOW WE BUILD

SKYSCRAPERS

HOW WE BUILD

SKYSCRAPERS

Philip Sauvain

GEC **GARRETT EDUCATIONAL CORPORATION**

© GEC Garrett Educational Corporation

Edited by Rebecca Stefoff

GEC Garrett Educational Corporation

U.S.A. text © 1990 by Garrett Educational Corporation
First Published in the United States in 1990 by
Garrett Educational Corporation, 130 East 13th Street,
Ada, OK 74820

First Published 1989 by Macmillan Children's Books,
England, © Macmillan Publishers Limited 1989

Manufactured in the United States of America

Library of Congress Cataloging-in-Publication Data

Sauvain, Philip Arthur.
    Skyscrapers / Philip Sauvain.
    p.   cm. - (How we build)
    Includes index.
    Summary: Describes the history, planning, and construction of
skyscrapers.
    ISBN 0-944483-78-X
    1. Skyscrapers-Design and construction-Juvenile literature.
[1. Skyscrapers-Design and construction.] I. Title II. Series.
TH1615.S28   1990
690-dc20   90-40358
                                                               CIP
                                                                AC

> **Note to the reader**
> In this book there are some words in the text which are printed in **bold** type.
> This shows that the word is listed in the glossary on page 46. The glossary
> gives a brief explanation of words that may be new to you.

Contents

Why build skyscrapers?

Millions of people all over the world live or work in the buildings we call skyscrapers. Skyscrapers tower over the land in cities as far apart as New York, Moscow, Tokyo, Rio de Janeiro, Cape Town, and Sydney. Skilled **architects** plan and design these skyscrapers. The architects work with **structural engineers** who make sure that, however tall the skyscrapers may be, they will be structurally sound.

Skyscrapers are most often found in the centers of crowded cities, where land for new buildings is scarce and therefore expensive. The only way to get a large building into a small space is to build upwards. In Hong Kong, where land is very precious, even the buildings in new towns outside the city are built as skyscrapers.

Offices

Office buildings have to be in the heart of the city so that the companies who own them, or rent space in them, can be near the others with whom they do business. It is not convenient for a company to have its offices scattered around in different buildings. In a skyscraper, all its workers can be under the same roof. A skyscraper can provide office space for thousands of working people on a relatively small amount of land.

▼ Vacant land in a city center can be used for a public park or for a car park. It can also be used for shops, offices, or apartment buildings. The taller the buildings, the greater the number of people who can live or work there.

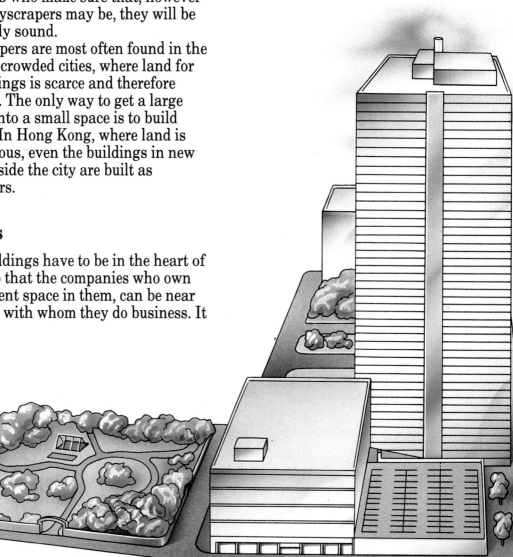

Homes

Skyscrapers also provide homes. Living in an apartment in a skyscraper, close to the center of a city, makes it easy for people to get to work. The apartment is handy for shops, theaters, restaurants, and sport centers. Airports and rail and bus stations are within easy reach. City people may spend most of their lives living and working in very tall buildings.

Learning about skyscrapers

In this book you will learn more about skyscrapers. You will see how they are built and how they differ from one another. You will also find out what problems architects and engineers have to solve in order to build them.

▼ The skyscrapers in New York City in the United States make it possible for millions of people to work within an area of a few square miles (kilometers).

Tall buildings of the past

Some massive cathedrals and towers of castles built in Europe 900 years ago are still standing. One such tower is the Torre Asinelli, which was built in 1109 in Bologna, in Italy. The builders of this structure understood that the walls of the tower had to be thicker at its base, because this foundation would have to support the entire weight of the structure.

The people who built the Leaning Tower of Pisa 800 years ago built foundations for their structure, but they did not take into account the soft ground on which they were building. The ground was not solid enough to support the tower, which began to sink and tilt under its own weight.

Starting at the bottom

Builders who want to reach for the sky must first look downward. They must find out what kind of ground they are building on. A tall building needs very firm foundations that will not sink or shift. If the ground has no solid rock in it on which to build the foundations, the builders must dig deep into the ground and build a support for their foundations that is as hard and immovable as rock. Otherwise, their towers will lean like the Leaning Tower of Pisa.

Supporting the walls

In times past, the high walls of churches and other large stone buildings sometimes collapsed under their own weight. Then builders discovered that they could prop up the walls by building supports up against them. These **buttresses** kept the main walls from falling outward.

Smaller buildings were often built by starting with a wooden frame. The builders filled the spaces in the frames with mud and plaster to make the walls. Heavy wooden beams were fixed in place on top of the frame to support the ceilings and the roof. The frame, not the walls, bore the weight of the roof and kept the house from falling down.

▲ The Leaning Tower of Pisa in Italy has one side that is 180 feet (55 meters) high. The other side is 177 feet (54 meters) high. The tower leans 16.4 feet (5 meters) out of the perpendicular.

▶ Medieval stonemasons carved buttresses to give extra support to the walls of cathedrals.

8

Build a buttress

You will need: three rectangles of stiff cardboard and some wooden building blocks.

1 Make a model of a simple building as shown.

card

2 Test the strength of the walls and roof by placing wooden blocks on the roof, one by one, until the building falls down. Do the walls fall inward or outward?

3 Now try using the blocks to build two buttresses on either side of the building to prop up the walls.

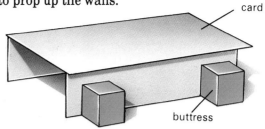
card

buttress

4 Test the strength of the building again. Put blocks on top of the roof, one by one, until the walls fall down. Which way do they fall? How do the buttresses help to stop the walls from falling?

The first skyscrapers

From the middle of the 1800s, engineers in Europe had been experimenting with the use of iron and steel in buildings. Iron and steel were lighter and stronger than brick and stone, the materials which had previously been used in buildings, but which were not strong enough to support towering structures.

In 1860, a storehouse for boats that was built in Sheerness, in England, became the first iron-framed building in which the frame bore the whole weight of the structure. In the early 1880s, Gustave Eiffel used steel to strengthen the Statue of Liberty, which still stands at the entrance to New York Harbor. When he built the Eiffel Tower in Paris in 1889, it was the highest structure in the world. It remained the highest until 1930, showing what strength there was in a steel frame.

A city built from ashes

In 1871, a fire swept through the city of Chicago. Much of the city burned down and had to be rebuilt. Terrible though it was, this disaster happened at a time that gave architects an opportunity to design some of the world's first skyscrapers.

Elevators

The skyscrapers that were used to rebuild the city of Chicago would never have reached such great heights without the use of elevators. Steam-powered elevators were invented in 1857 but were too slow. The increasing use of electricity made possible the invention of a high-speed elevator in 1887. This meant that architects could design much higher buildings.

▼ The Chicago Fire of 1871 was the worst fire in American history. However, it meant that a new kind of city and some early skyscrapers could be built to replace the buildings that were destroyed by the fire.

Steel frames

Iron or steel frames were proving strong enough to bear the strain of the weight, or **load,** of a large building. In stone buildings, all the load was on the walls, but in metal-framed structures every part of the frame shared the load equally. This divided the total load so that each part of the frame had less weight to carry.

Steel was better than iron for use in building construction as it is a much stronger material. Until 1880, however, steel was very expensive. Then new production methods made it cheaper and more plentiful.

In 1885, the first metal-framed skyscraper, the Home Insurance Building, was built in Chicago in the United States. It was ten stories high and had an iron and steel frame.

Deep foundations

As buildings grew higher, engineers had to work out how deep to dig their foundations. They had to calculate the effect of the building's load on the frame and on the ground. The Woolworth Building, built in New York in 1913, amazed the world with its 60 stories. The foundations of the building, which was 761 feet (232 meters) high, reached 131 feet (40 meters) into the solid rock beneath New York City.

▲ The Woolworth Building in New York was the tallest skyscraper in the world until 1930. It is more highly ornamented than most skyscrapers today.

◀ The Eiffel Tower was once thought ugly, but is now one of the landmarks of Paris. It is 984 feet (300 meters) high. The frame was made from wrought iron, which is stronger than ordinary iron.

Types of skyscraper

The next time you visit a large city, take a look at its tall buildings. In what ways do they vary in shape and style? In what ways are they the same?

The simplest form of skyscraper is shaped like a rectangular box with a flat roof. Older skyscrapers were often topped with a graceful tower or spire. Recently, architects have experimented with many different shapes.

Skyscrapers may be rectangular, square, or triangular. They may be many-sided or arc-shaped and not at all symmetrical.

Australia Square Building   Trans-America Building

▲ Australia's tallest skyscraper, which is in Sydney, is round. The Trans-America Building in San Francisco is in the shape of a pyramid.

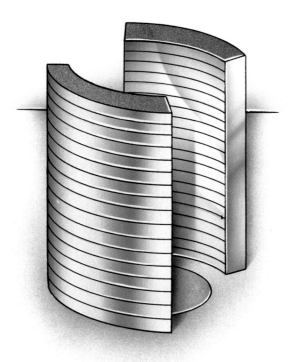

▲ The City Hall in Toronto, Canada, has curved walls.

How skyscrapers are built

Older skyscrapers, like the Woolworth and Empire State Buildings, have steel frames. Today, a frame is more often made by combining steel with concrete. Steel rods or wires are sunk into the concrete while it is soft. As the concrete hardens, it forms a very strong material called **reinforced concrete.**

Recent skyscrapers built in the United States often have a strong central inner tube, or **core,** made of reinforced concrete. The John Hancock Center in Chicago is built this way. The World Trade Center in New York City has an outer tube as well, instead of a steel or concrete frame. The world's tallest skyscraper, the Sears Tower in Chicago, is a cluster of nine tubes built together.

Shapes and styles

The most important factor in determining the shape of a skyscraper is the shape of the plot of land on which it is to be built. The 20-story Flatiron Building, erected in New York in 1902, is wedge-shaped because the building site was wedge-shaped. The slim, slab-shaped United Nations Building had to be squeezed between New York's First Avenue and the East River.

Skyscrapers may be built in unusual shapes and styles to meet special requirements or to make them stand out from other buildings. A group of Los Angeles hotels has shining walls of gold-tinted glass. Many skyscrapers have the upper stories set back to allow light into the street below, or to make space for roof gardens, restaurants, or tennis courts.

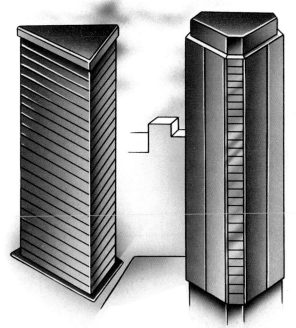

▲ The Flatiron Building in New York is triangular, and the National Westminster Tower in London has many sides.

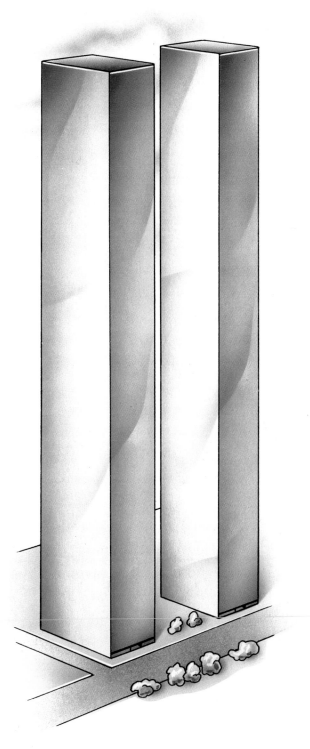

▲ The huge twin towers of the World Trade Center in New York are tall, wide, and square.

Plans for a skyscraper

Building a skyscraper costs a great deal of money. Every step in the process has to be carefully planned so the money is not wasted. Before the architects can even begin to make their designs, they need to ask a great many questions. How do the owners want the skyscraper to look? What do they intend to use it for? How many people will live or work there? What is the site like? What local laws will affect the building? How much money is available?

Once they have gathered all the information they need, the architects make detailed drawings of the skyscraper design. When the owners are satisfied with the design, the plans must be approved by the authorities in the city where the skyscraper is to be built. Without gaining **planning permission,** the builders chosen to do the work cannot start to build a new skyscraper.

Finding out about the site

The architects can see for themselves the shape of the site. It is the job of the structural engineers to find out about the soil below the site. Is the rock firm and solid, or soft? Does it absorb water easily?

To get the answers, the engineers drill holes called **boreholes** deep into the ground and extract samples of rock for testing. Their findings help them decide what sort of foundations the skyscraper they are planning will need to support its great weight.

Architects collect information about the weather conditions on the site. They consider the style of buildings nearby and how the new building will look alongside them. They decide which materials to use to build the skyscraper. Will it be cheaper to build the frame of the skyscraper out of reinforced concrete or steel?

▶ Architects prepare plans showing exactly what the skyscraper will look like. The authorities will want to know how a new skyscraper will change the look of their city.

▼ Before a skyscraper can be built, a surveyor has to make a study of the site. Special features are noted and measurements taken.

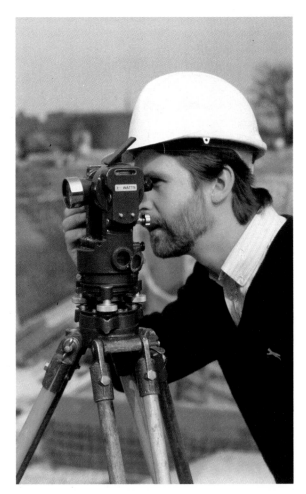

Choosing a builder

Once the architects have had their plans approved by the owners and by the city planning authorities, they can choose a builder. They ask several firms of builders to say what they would charge to build the skyscraper. The builders have to work out the cost of building materials and of hiring labor. How many workers will they need, and how long will it take them to do the job? They will want to make a profit, too. The builders submit a written **estimate** of these costs to the architects. The firm that gives the best estimate usually wins the contract to build the skyscraper.

▶ The architects' detailed plans tell the builders exactly what to do. They show the position of every door, wall, and window in every room and on every floor. They show where bathrooms, corridors, elevators, stairs, pipes, and power cables are to go.

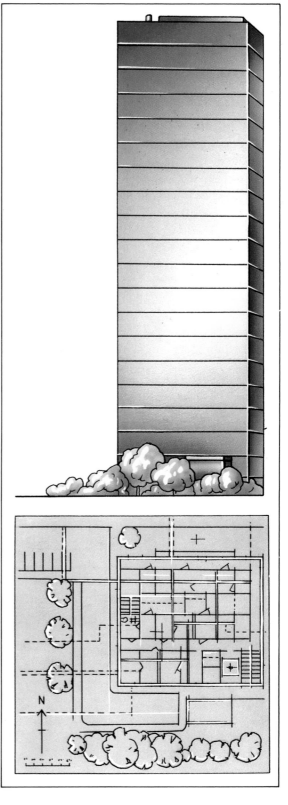

Planning problems

Imagine what it must be like to design a skyscraper with 100 floors and offices for 50,000 people! A large team or architects spends months working out detailed plans for each of the 100 floors. They may have to fit shops, theaters, swimming pools, and gymnasiums into their plans, as well as offices and apartments. The architects have to make sure that people inside the building are neither too warm nor too cold, whatever the weather is like outside. People must be able to move easily from one floor to another. The higher the skyscraper, the more problems there are for the architects to solve.

Avoiding dangers

Structural engineers have to consider every possible danger that could affect the skyscraper or the 50,000 people inside.

What would happen if the building caught fire? There are fire escapes, of course, but a fire that blocked the main exits of a skyscraper could end in a horrifying disaster. However, steel and concrete do not burn. The use of fireproof materials can prevent a fire in one part of the building from spreading.

A sprinkler system may be built into a skyscraper and connected to the building's water supply. The system of sprinklers is activated when it detects smoke or a sudden rise in temperature. Designers plan stairs inside a skyscraper that can be used as an alternative to elevators as well as allowing for plenty of possible exits from the building.

In parts of the world like Japan, Mexico, and California, earthquakes are a constant danger. Buildings in such places have to be specially strengthened so that they will not fall easily. Scientists are called in to experiment with new designs for structures that can withstand being shaken during an earthquake.

Buildings and people

A new skyscraper can create problems for the people in the buildings nearby. They may think it is ugly, or it may spoil their view or block out their light. For this reason, architects and engineers have to show their plans to a great many people and listen to their comments.

Skyscrapers can even get in the way of aircraft. Pilots must be careful when landing or taking off in places like Hong Kong, where the flight path takes them near many tall buildings.

▲ In 1985, an earthquake destroyed part of the center of Mexico City. Twenty thousand people were killed, and about 50,000 homes were lost. The collapse of many tall buildings added to the death toll.

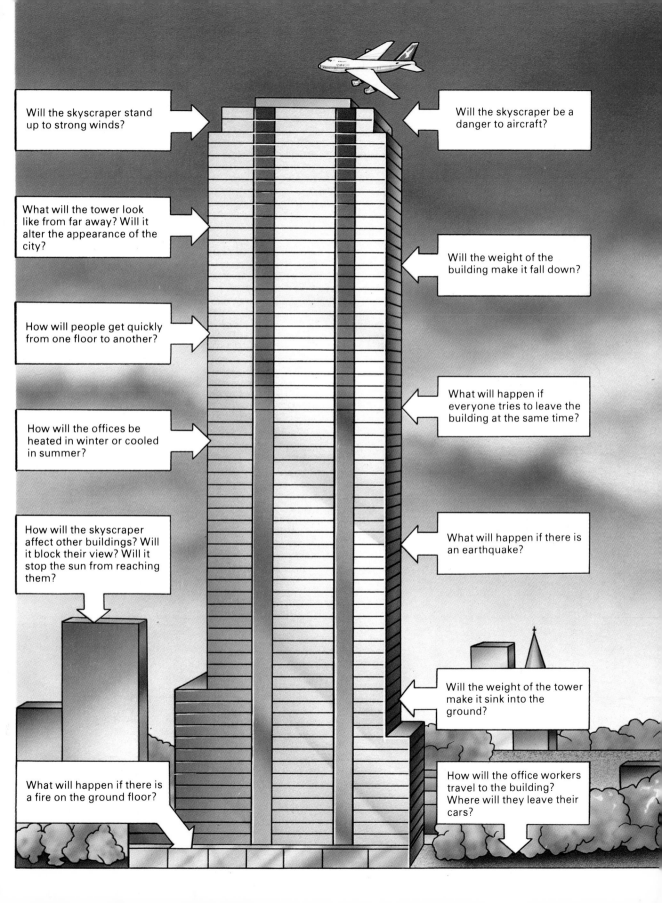

Foundations

Have you ever stood on a beach and felt yourself sink into the sand? The heavier you are, the deeper you sink. Just imagine what would happen to the sand if a hundred people stood on your shoulders! Yet if you were standing on solid rock, you would not sink at all.

Architects building a skyscraper have to start by giving it a firm foundation, a foundation like rock, not like sand. Some skyscrapers are built on huge slabs of concrete known as **rafts.** Others are built on columns of steel or concrete called **piles,** or **piers.** The piles are firmly attached to the hard rock that lies beneath the surface of the ground. The foundations of some buildings may consist of a concrete raft built on top of steel and concrete piles.

Solid rock

The best place on which to build a skyscraper is a site where solid rock, or **bedrock,** lies reasonably near the surface. Bedrock is the hard rock that forms part of the earth's crust. It is so hard that it can support any weight. Many of New York's skyscrapers stand on piles that are driven through layers of earth into the bedrock below Manhattan Island. Some of the piles go down 100 feet (30 meters) or more.

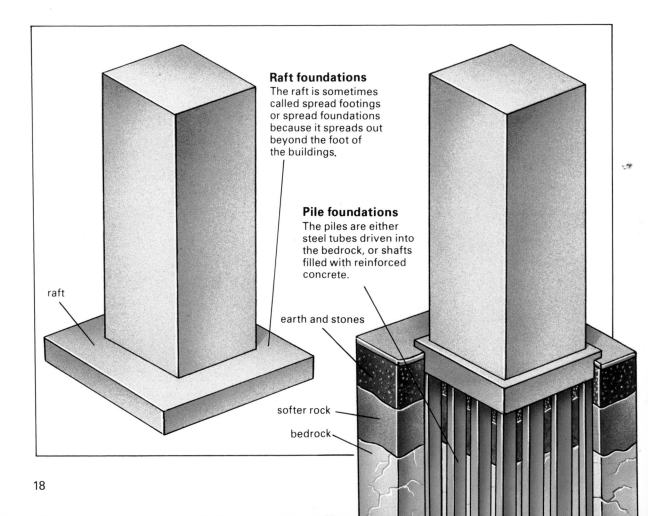

Raft foundations
The raft is sometimes called spread footings or spread foundations because it spreads out beyond the foot of the buildings.

Pile foundations
The piles are either steel tubes driven into the bedrock, or shafts filled with reinforced concrete.

raft

earth and stones

softer rock

bedrock

Piles

The piles that support skyscrapers can be made from steel or from reinforced concrete. Builders use huge machines known as pile drivers to pound the slender steel piles into the ground.

Concrete piles are made by drilling holes down into the bedrock and filling the holes with wet concrete. The concrete sets to form solid legs or pillars in the ground. Foundation piles are like the roots of a tree. They anchor the skyscraper to the ground so that it will not fall.

▶ Operating like a huge hammer, the pile driver drives piles deep into the ground with repeated heavy blows.

Building foundations

You will need: a plastic tray, modeling clay, some sand, some wooden blocks, 6 short sticks of equal length, a sheet of paper, and a stiff sheet of cardboard.

1 Line the bottom of the tray with a thick layer of clay, to form the bedrock. Then fill it with sand, to make the ground of the building site.

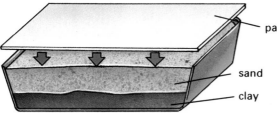

paper

sand

clay

2 Lay the sheet of paper on top. Try to build a skyscraper with the building blocks. Are the foundations firm?

3 Now try pushing the sticks (the piles) through the ground until they stick fast in the clay. Make sure the tops of the piles are level. They should just show above the ground.

4 Lay the sheet of cardboard, which represents a slab of concrete, on top of the piles. Now see if the foundations are firm enough to let you build your skyscraper.

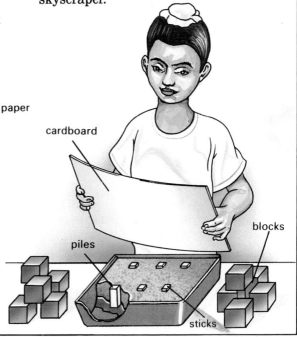

cardboard

blocks

piles

sticks

19

Building on soft ground

People used to think that no one could ever build skyscrapers in cities like London. Instead of hard rock below the surface of the ground, the land under London consists of soft layers of clay and gravel. However, London now has several skyscrapers. Architects and engineers have shown that tall buildings can be built even on soft ground.

A concrete raft

Piles alone do not make strong enough foundations for a skyscraper if there is no bedrock to support them. Instead, the builders lay down a thick slab of reinforced concrete to serve as a raft. As the raft covers a much larger area than the building that will eventually stand on it, it distributes the weight of the skyscraper over a large part of the building site.

The size and thickness of the raft are not left to chance. Using computers, structural engineers can calculate exactly how strong the foundations must be to support a building of a given height and weight. Skyscrapers do not weigh as much as they once did. Stone, bricks, and iron have been replaced by much lighter building materials such as aluminum.

▶ Britain's tallest skyscraper is the National Westminster Tower in London. Completed in 1979, it is 600 feet (183 meters) high. It has 49 floors and 21 elevators.

Building a skyscraper in London

A reinforced concrete raft provided the main foundations for the National Westminster Tower in London. The builders began by clearing the site using bulldozers, and then scraping it flat. They dug deep trenches to carry away the water drained from the site. Using excavators, they hollowed out a huge hole, about 180 feet (55 meters) square and 16 feet (5 meters) deep. Then the builders placed about 2500 tons of steel rods upright inside the hole and filled it with wet concrete. They laid wooden boards on top. These boards held the concrete down while it dried and set solid around the steel rods. This enormous raft made a firm base for London's tallest building.

▼ The builders poured liquid concrete onto upright steel rods to make the reinforced concrete raft for the National Westminster Tower. The soft clay underneath London makes it difficult to build skyscrapers. Most tall buildings in London stand on concrete rafts like this one.

A strong frame

Even if the foundations of a skyscraper are strong, there is still a danger that the weight of the building may make it collapse. For this reason, a skyscraper needs a strong frame to hold it together. The first skyscrapers built in Chicago and New York had iron and steel frames. The frames not only supported the weight of the roof, floors, walls, windows, and furnishings, but also the weight of the people who occupied the buildings. Many skyscrapers are still built using steel and concrete frames.

Raising the frame

A frame is raised by fitting lengths of steel together to make a rigid, box-like structure. There are upright columns of steel, long steel beams, or **girders,** and shorter cross beams which join them all together. They are lifted into place by giant cranes. Where the sections of the framework overlap, steel pins or bolts, called **rivets,** are driven through them by riveting machines, fastening one section to another. Where two sections meet end to end, they must be **welded** together. This is done by heating the edges of the metals so that they melt and merge into one another, creating a strong joint and a continuous surface. The finished frame is often called the **shell** of a building.

▶ An enormous amount of steel is needed to make the columns, girders, and beams in the frame of a skyscraper.

▼ The strength of a steel frame depends upon the strength of its joints. The girders used to be joined to the columns and to other girders with rivets. Now, most joints are welded.

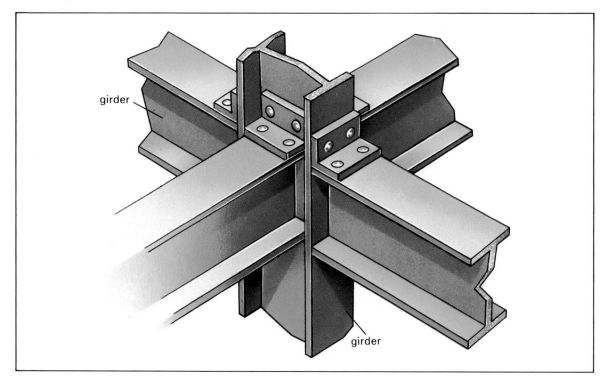

girder

girder

Towers of steel

The chief advantage of constructing a skyscraper on a steel frame is that the frame, not the walls, carries most of the weight of the building. The walls only serve to keep out the heat, cold, wind, and rain. The walls can be thin and can be make of quite light materials. Many new office buildings appear to be built entirely of glass or aluminum.

It is also easier to make a skyscraper fireproof if it is built around a frame. There is no need for wooden beams. Walls, floors, and ceilings can all be made of fireproof materials.

Another advantage is that steel-frame skyscrapers are quicker to build than other buildings of the same size. Before one team of builders has finished raising the frame, another team can start attaching the outer walls to the parts of the frame that have already been erected. Meanwhile, other workers such as plumbers and electricians, can start work inside the building, without waiting until the roof is in place.

Ready-made walls

The sheets of glass or panels of aluminum that are used for the walls are called **cladding.** The use of cladding, which can be made of a wide range of materials, greatly speeds up the building of the skyscraper. The panels are manufactured, well before they are needed, to the exact size shown in the architects' drawings. They are, in other words, **prefabricated.** Then they are delivered to the building site by truck and lifted into position by cranes. Building workers fasten the cladding securely to the framework of the building.

◄ Can you pick out the frame of the Richard Daley Center in Chicago?

24

Making a frame

You will need: large and small interlocking plastic building bricks and wall panels of the type shown.

1 Build a model frame like the one in the diagram. Use long building bricks for the girders and cross beams, and smaller bricks for the four columns.

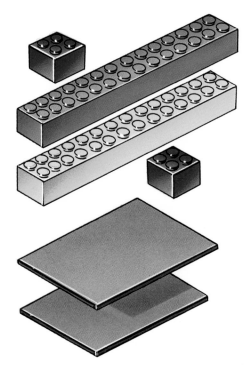

2 Each time you add new cross beams to the frame, join the bricks securely to those above and below them, and to those on the same level.

3 How strong is your frame? Now fit the wall panels. Fit them to the top of the frame before you fit them to the bottom. Do they have any effect on the frame? Do they make the frame stronger or weaker?

Reinforced concrete

Today, many tall buildings are built with reinforced concrete frames. The girders, columns, and beams are all made of reinforced concrete instead of steel. However, concrete would not make a strong enough frame for a skyscraper if it were not reinforced with steel.

Steel and concrete

A concrete beam can be squeezed, or **compressed,** without breaking. However, it will soon snap if it is stretched or put under **tension.** Steel stands up well to both compression and tension. This is why the concrete beams used in buildings are strengthened with steel.

To strengthen concrete, builders lay steel rods inside temporary molds of the correct size and shape, known as the **formwork** or **shuttering.** Then wet concrete is poured into the shuttering and is allowed to dry and set hard. The steel rods give the concrete the strength it needs to prevent it from breaking under tension. Sometimes the steel itself is stretched, or stressed, to make an even stronger, lighter material called **pre-stressed concrete.**

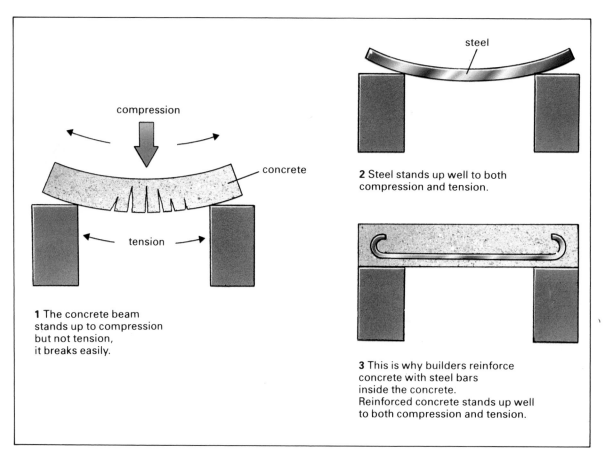

compression

concrete

tension

1 The concrete beam stands up to compression but not tension, it breaks easily.

steel

2 Steel stands up well to both compression and tension.

3 This is why builders reinforce concrete with steel bars inside the concrete. Reinforced concrete stands up well to both compression and tension.

Using concrete

Reinforced concrete is used for the foundations of skyscrapers, as well as for the beams, columns, and girders that make concrete frames. It may also be used in other ways. Sometimes concrete is poured into molds to build a strong, hollow core at the center of the building. Reinforced concrete beams radiate from this central core to support the floors of the skyscraper.

Raising concrete floors

Some reinforced concrete buildings are constructed by casting the concrete in its eventual position on the building. Alternatively, sections of the building may be cast in a factory and be assembled on the building site.

Recently, however, builders have found it quicker to use the **lift slab** method of construction. They start by erecting upright columns. Then the concrete for each floor is mixed and cast in shuttering on the ground. When dry and hard, the floors are stacked in order on the ground, ready to be hoisted, as they are needed, to the height required.

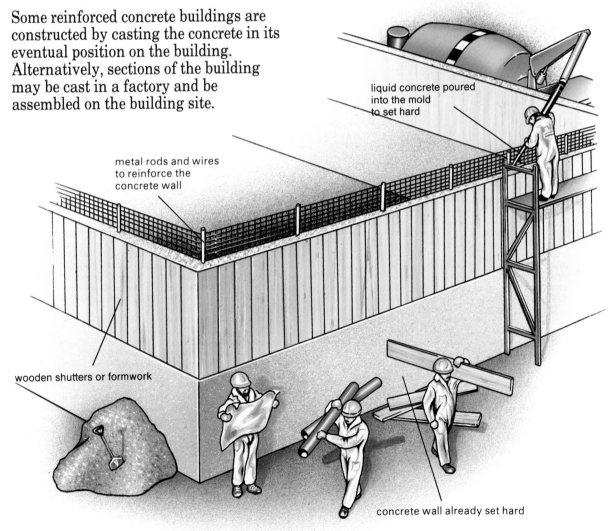

liquid concrete poured into the mold to set hard

metal rods and wires to reinforce the concrete wall

wooden shutters or formwork

concrete wall already set hard

Skyscrapers with a core

If you watch a skyscraper being built, you may be surprised to see the workers start by erecting a huge concrete column, not a steel or concrete frame. This reinforced concrete core is the spine of the skyscraper, holding it upright.

A hollow tube

Although the core looks solid, it is usually hollow, like a tube. The space inside the core can be used to provide essential services for the people who live and work in the skyscraper. They must have light and heat, telephones, water, and air conditioning. Most of all, they need to get from one floor to another. The wires, cables, pipes, and elevators that keep life going inside a skyscraper can all be installed safely within the building's fireproof hollow core.

The floor space between the core and the outer walls is called the hull. For this reason, skyscrapers built around a central core are known as **hull and core** skyscrapers. The outer **curtain walls** are of cladding, usually made from light materials like glass or aluminum.

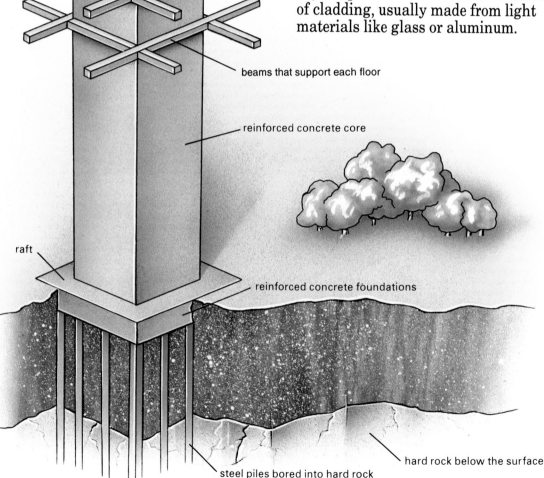

beams that support each floor

reinforced concrete core

raft

reinforced concrete foundations

steel piles bored into hard rock

hard rock below the surface

Plenty of space

Each floor of a hull and core skyscraper is laid on concrete beams that reach out from the central core. The skyscraper rises into the sky almost like a tree, with the foundation piles as its roots, the core as its trunk, and the beams as its branches. The great advantage of this design is that it creates plenty of floor space. There are no inside columns like the ones found in skyscrapers built on a steel or concrete frame. There are no columns at all between the core and the curtain walls. As a result, the floor space can be divided up in any way that is convenient. The rooms on each floor are bigger, and more people get a view from their windows than would be the case in a skyscraper built around a frame.

▲ The Tour Maine-Montparnasse in Paris is a hull and core structure. At 656 feet (200 meters) high, it is one of Europe's tallest skyscrapers.

◀ The thick central column of a hull and core skyscraper is easy to see when it is being built.

29

When the wind blows

When a strong wind blows across Lake Michigan, some of Chicago's skyscrapers begin to sway. The movement may be slight, but it is enough to make chandeliers inside the buildings swing from side to side.

High winds present more of a problem to structural engineers today than they did in the past. This is because skyscrapers have become lighter as they have become taller.

Braced against the wind

Architects and engineers have to make sure that the structure of a new skyscraper is well braced against the wind. If it sways too much, the people inside may suffer from seasickness, just as they might on a moving ship. The designers of the John Hancock Center, in Chicago, fixed huge crossed beams to the sides of the building. These beams help it to withstand the force of high winds. Such beams are called **cross braces.**

Testing the model

Fortunately for the owners, engineers now have ways of predicting how strong winds could affect a new skyscraper. Before the skyscraper is built, they make an exact scale model of it from the architect's plans. Then they test the model in a special room, where an electric fan can be made to simulate various wind speeds. This room is known as a **wind tunnel.** The engineers can set the fan to produce light winds, gales, and even hurricanes. Special instruments on the sides of the model,

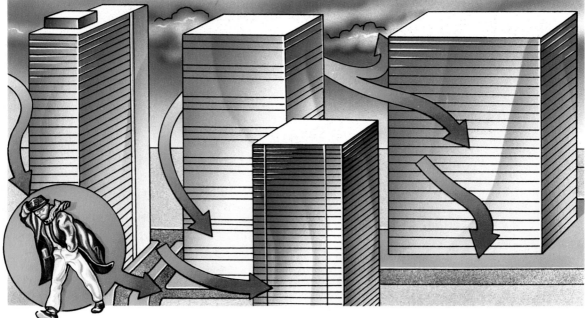

▲ Skyscrapers block the path of the wind. This forces the wind between the buildings where it blows much harder.

called **pressure sensors,** measure the effects of the wind.

From these tests, engineers can judge how badly the skyscraper would be likely to sway in a high wind. They can see, from any damage to the model, what damage wind might do to the skyscraper. The tests show them whether they need to make changes in their designs to give the skyscraper greater wind resistance than the model has demonstrated.

▶ **You can see the steel cross-bracing on the sides of the John Hancock Center, in the center of the picture. The tower is narrower at the top than at the bottom, which also helps it to withstand the force of the wind.**

Wind tunnel tests

You will need: about 20 building blocks and an electric hair dryer.

1 Build your own model skyscraper with the building blocks. Set it in the middle of a table.

2 Switch on the electric hair dryer, and turn it up to its highest speed.

3 Start your wind tunnel test some distance away from the model. Does the skyscraper move?

4 Make the wind blow harder by moving the hair dryer nearer the model. Move it around so that the wind hits the model from different directions. Do these changes affect the model in any way?

5 If your skyscraper blows down easily, see what you can do to the model to brace it more firmly against the wind.

6 Repeat your tests until your skyscraper can resist the air from the hair dryer.

Safety first: Treat electrical appliances with care and common sense. Never use a hair dryer near water.

Living and working

Would you be scared to live or work in a skyscraper? Some people are. Lots of people are afraid of heights, and others hate being enclosed in small spaces. Life in a skyscraper is not easy if you are nervous about looking out of the windows or traveling in the elevators.

Getting up and down

In buildings with ten or more stories, the only sensible way to get up and down is by elevator. Even so, if the elevator stops at every floor it can take a long time to reach the higher floors.

Skyscrapers usually have express elevators that make very few stops. The World Trade Center in New York has 23 express elevators. They take you straight from the first floor to one of the three "skylobbies", or transfer points. The skylobbies are on the 44th, 78th, and 107th floors. They help to divide each of the twin towers into an upper, middle, and lower section. Office workers take the express lift to the skylobby for the section of the building they wish to reach. Then local lifts take them up or down to the floor where they work.

Keeping cool

Air conditioning keeps skyscrapers at a comfortable temperature for the people inside. It brings in a steady supply of fresh air for people to breathe. The windows are never opened.

Keeping the building cool is a bigger problem than keeping it warm. The

▲ Many modern skyscrapers have their elevators, pipes, and cables on the outside of the building.

▼ Air conditioning units keep skyscrapers at an even temperature, whatever the weather is like outside.

warmth from people's bodies, and from machines like computers, creates a lot of heat. So does the sun on glass walls. The heat rises up through the building as if it were a huge chimney. If the doors at the street level were allowed to stand open, the air coming in could cause a powerful draft to blow like a gale through the building. This is why you often see revolving doors at the entrance to a skyscraper.

Living in the sky

What is it like to live in a skyscraper? For some people it is wonderful to live high in the sky, above the noise and dust of city streets. People will pay a great deal of money for a **penthouse** on the roof. There they can have a garden, fresh air, and a bird's-eye view of the city stretching beneath them.

There are drawbacks, however, to life in an ordinary skyscraper apartment. Children may have little space to play. Adults may become lonely because they do not know their neighbors. For old people, it is a long way down to the street. Other people miss seeing trees and grass. Although some people have balconies, and may fill them with flowers, others live so high in the clouds that they have to use the telephone to find out if it is raining in the street below!

▼ One hundred years ago, most city people lived and worked in buildings with fewer than five floors.

▼ Many millions of people in many different countries now live in tall apartment buildings. Life is very different in a skyscraper than it is close to the ground.

City planning

When skyscrapers were first built, each one was a wonder in itself. Now most people realize that even skyscrapers should fit in with the buildings around them. Most cities have laws to say what can and cannot be built. These laws may set a limit on the height of future buildings.

Letting in the sunshine

New York City passed laws that affected new buildings more than 70 years ago. In 1915 New Yorkers grew angry as they saw the Equitable Building rise higher and higher. The finished skyscraper gave its owners an enormous amount of office space. When the size of the floor space on all the floors was added together, it was more than 30 times the size of the land on which the building stood. However, its walls rose straight up from the street, so that people down below were always in its shade.

There were so many complaints that, in 1916, the city authorities passed a law to control the way high buildings were to be built in the future. Since that time, architects have had to get planning permission before starting work. They have had to make sure that the upper part of a skyscraper was set far enough back to let light reach buildings nearby and streets below. A skyscraper could not be built at all if its total floor space amounted to more than 12 times the size of the building site. Also, gardens and terraces are often incorporated into the design of a new skyscraper to make sure

▲ When the Equitable Building was built, New Yorkers saw the effect skyscrapers had on buildings around them and on people in the street.

that the building provides a pleasant environment for the people who live or work in it.

Good to look at

Although everyone hopes that new skyscrapers will be good to look at, people rarely agree on what looks best! Some people admire the square towers of the

World Trade Center, while others think the box-like shapes of the towers look bland. Look at page 40. What do you think?

The Seagram Building in New York has been praised for its elegance. However, this building also has its critics. Some people have said that some features of the design make it more decorative than useful. It has been argued, for example, that the windows of the building are too far away from the areas where people are at work. Architects have to find a balance between how a skyscraper will look and its use.

▼ New York's Chrysler Building, with it tower that symbolizes the rising sun, was completed in 1930. When it was nearly finished workers pushed a steel spire through the dome to make it higher than a rival skyscraper in Wall Street.

▼ The architects Ludwig Miles van der Rohe and Philip Johnson designed New York's Seagram Building.

Changing skylines

What will skyscrapers look like a hundred years from now? Will the people of the 21st century want to live and work in such high buildings? Already some tall apartment buildings in Britain and the United States have been pulled down because they were unsafe, or because people did not choose to live in them.

However, with more and more people in the world and less and less spare land for building, there may be little choice. If land is needed for growing food, buildings will have to spread upward, not outward. Whatever doubts we may have about the future, architects will surely be designing new skyscrapers.

Skyscrapers of tomorrow

Among the possible designs architects have prepared for a new Chicago Trade Center building, there are two that would make it far taller than any skyscraper yet seen. The first is for a skyscraper 2460 feet (750 meters) high, with 210 stories. The second would be twice as high, with 500 stories. This one would be built of triangular tubes.

As long ago as 1956, one of the United States' best-known architects, Frank Lloyd Wright, produced plans for a building 528 stories high. People living at the top of his "Mile High" skyscraper would probably not even be having the same weather as people in the street below! Yet architects and engineers agree that they now have the knowledge, skills, and materials that would make it possible to build a skyscraper twice as high as the one Wright designed. More than 200,000 people could live in it. It would be like a whole city inside one building. It could include offices, schools, shops, medical services, and sports and entertainment facilities. People could live most of their lives without going outside.

◄ Are these the homes of the future? People plug their apartments, or capsules, into the Nakagin Capsule Tower in Tokyo. They can take them with them when they move to another city!

New York past and present

From the very beginning, the development of skyscrapers was especially dramatic in New York City. In 1865, Manhattan Island, at the heart of the city, was mainly a place of three, four, or five-story buildings. It was growing fast, however. Every inch of land had become valuable.

The solid rock beneath the surface of the ground made Manhattan a good place in which to build skyward. Fifty years later, the lower end of the island, where most of the banks, offices, and government buildings were situated, was a mass of skyscrapers. That was in 1915. Today, buildings like the World Trade Center have changed the skyline of New York City yet again.

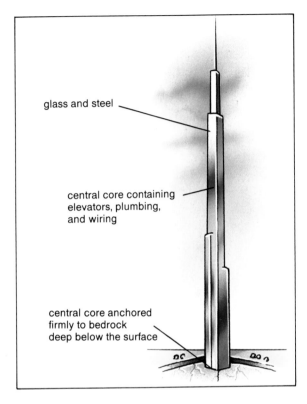

glass and steel

central core containing elevators, plumbing, and wiring

central core anchored firmly to bedrock deep below the surface

▲ Frank Lloyd Wright's "Mile-High" skyscraper.

▼ New York City in the early 1900s, with the Brooklyn Bridge in the foreground.

The Empire State Building

The tallest steel-frame skyscraper in the world is the Empire State Building in New York City. It became the world's tallest building on its completion in 1931 and remained so until 1973. New Yorkers called it "The Cathedral of the Skies." Many people think it is still the greatest building achievement of the 20th century.

The Empire State Building's massive frame was made by riveting together 60,000 tons of steel beams, columns, and girders. The frame had to be very strong because the total weight of the building is 365,000 tons. Much of this weight comes from the walls, which are made of stone.

Twenty months

It took 3500 workers, working day and night for 20 months, to build the Empire State Building. Fourteen men were killed while working on the project. New Yorkers were amazed to see the building grow at the rate of almost a story a day. If they went away for two weeks, they would find the building ten stories higher when they returned!

The use of a steel frame had transformed the whole process of erecting large buildings. Long before the frame was completed, work had begun on the floors below. Plumbers, carpenters, and electricians started to do their jobs without waiting until the walls were all in place. They worked at various jobs on different floors.

The Empire State Building today

The Empire State Building was one of the wonders of the world when it was opened in 1931. The view of New York from the top floors was spectacular and is still one of the city's main attractions. The walls appear to be made of solid limestone and granite, but only the outer covering is of stone. Its weight does have one big advantage. It makes the building so heavy that it sways only one and one-half inches (four centimeters) at the top, even in a high wind.

◀ At one stage during the construction of the Empire State Building, it was taking less than four days to make the steel, form it into girders, and attach the girders in place at the top of the building.

▶ The Empire State Building today.

Fact panel

* The foundations of the Empire State Building were begun in October 1929.

* The building was opened on May 1, 1931.

* The height of the main building is 1250 feet (381 meters).

* The height to the top of the television aerial is 1473 feet (440 meters).

* The Empire State Building has 102 stories and over 6000 windows.

* There are 73 elevators and nearly 7 miles (11 kilometers) of elevator shafts.

* The building provides office space for 20,000 people.

Fact panel

* One and a half million people visit the Empire State Building every year.

* There are nearly 2000 steps to the top of the tower.

* It takes half an hour to walk down them from top to bottom but only a minute traveling in the elevator.

* You can see for 50 miles (80 kilometers) from the top of the tower on a clear day.

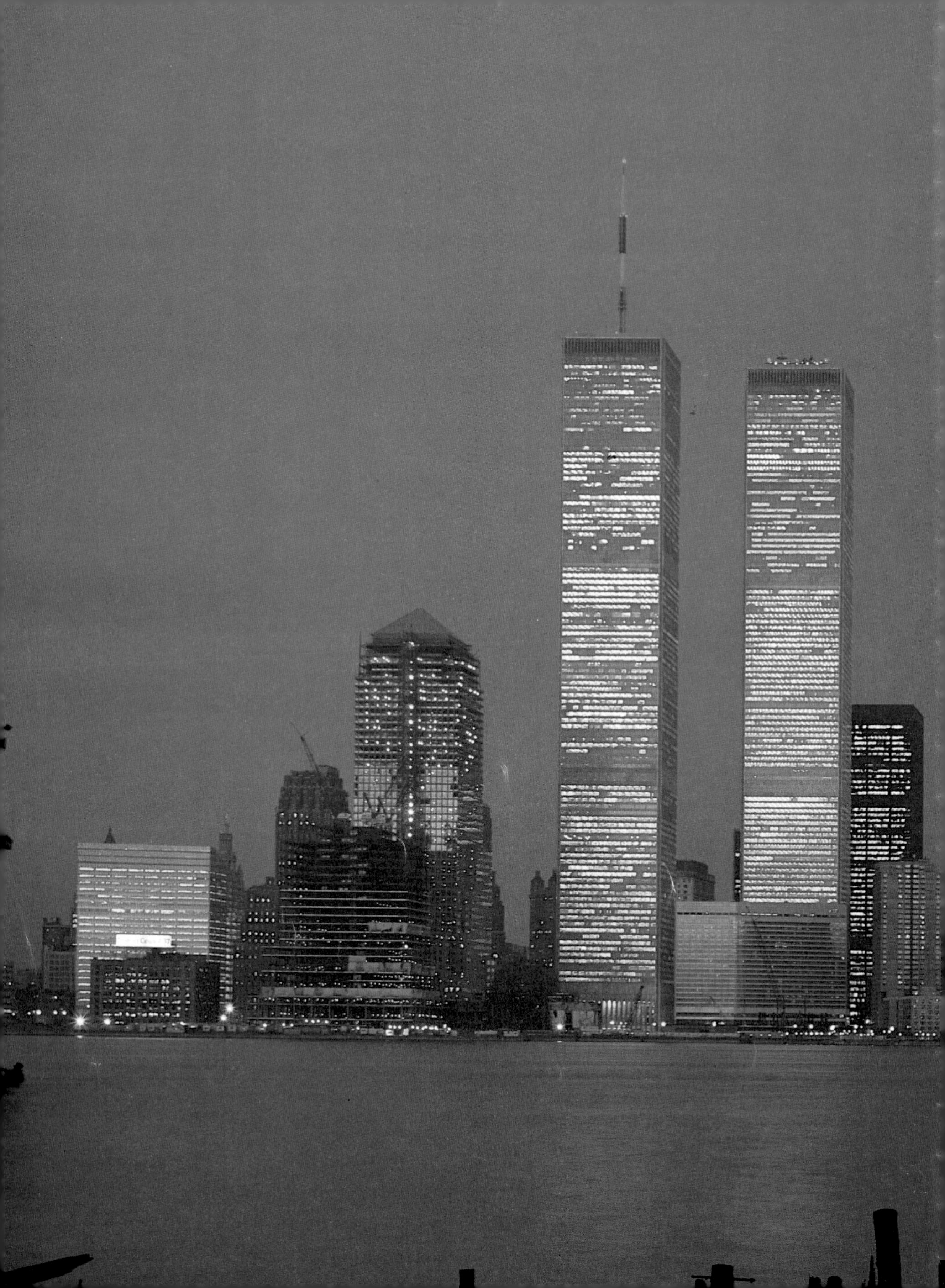

The World Trade Center

When the World Trade Center was built in New York City in 1973, it was 112 feet (34 meters) higher than the Empire State Building. For one year it was the tallest skyscraper in the world. Then the Sears Tower in Chicago, 92 feet (28 meters) higher still, took first place. The Sears Tower remains the tallest building in the world, but the World Trade Center still holds one world record. It has twice as much office space as any other skyscraper in the world.

◄ The twin towers of the World Trade Center dominate the New York City skyline. Fifty thousand people work in the Center which is visited by nearly half a million people each day.

Building the Center

The World Trade Center was built in lower Manhattan, overlooking the Statue of Liberty. When the Center was still in the planning stage, experts carried out wind tunnel tests on a model of the building. When the model skyscraper shook badly in the wind, the architects had no choice but to design a totally new type of structure.

They built the Center as two hull and core skyscrapers, each with a very strong square tower as its core. In addition, they built hundreds of slim columns all the way around the four sides of each tower. This made the walls strong enough to support the weight of the building. Each tower is like a huge, square tube with another tube, the core, in the middle. Inside each core are the elevators and other services.

Fact panel

* The World Trade Center is 1362 feet (415 meters) high. It is the highest building in New York.

* Its twin towers are called One World Trade Center and Two World Trade Center.

* Each of the towers is 110 stories high.

* The area of each floor equals more than one acre.

* There are 43,600 windows in the twin towers.

The Sears Tower

The Sears Tower in Chicago is 1454 feet (443 meters) high, with 110 stories. It is the world's tallest skyscraper. Add on the extra height of its television aerial, and it stands nearly one-third of a mile high.

As it is mainly an office building, the designers took great care to make it comfortable to work in. The glass in its 16,000 windows is tinted bronze, to reduce the glare from the sun. The tinted glass keeps the building at a pleasant temperature, too. Otherwise the sun pouring in through all those windows could turn it into a hothouse! To make the Sears Tower handsome as well as comfortable, black aluminum cladding was used on the outside walls.

Nine towers in one

The architects and engineers who designed the Sears Tower had to solve the special problems of building in Chicago, which is called "The Windy City." An unusual kind of structure was needed. Instead of building it with outer and inner tubes, like the World Trade Center, they built nine square tubes, or towers. These towers, each with a width of 74.5 feet (23 meters), form a huge square building, each side of which is 226 feet (69 meters) wide at the street level. Not all the towers are the same height, which makes the Sears Tower easy to recognize.

Solid strength

A number of factors contribute to the solid strength of the Sears Tower. The nine towers were given added strength by the choice of steel used to reinforce the concrete. The towers are also built in such a way that each one shares walls with one of the others.

This kind of construction also means that there are plenty of inside walls to support the weight of the floors above. The inner walls make the skyscraper so strong that the outer walls bear a comparatively light load. This sharing of the load meant that the architects could use large panes of glass, as well as aluminum, for the cladding.

▶ The Sears Tower under construction. The tallest tower in the world is the headquarters of one of the largest retail and mail order companies in the world, the Sears, Roebuck Company.

▲ The pattern of skyscrapers on the skyline makes it easy to tell great cities apart. The shape of the Sears Tower shows that this city is Chicago

▶ The Sears Tower has nine square tubes at ground level, seven tubes at the 51st floor level, and five tubes at the 67th floor lever, but only two tubes from the 90th floor to the top.

Fact panel

* The Sears Tower took four years to build between 1970 and 1974.

* At 1454 feet (443 meters) high, it is the tallest building in the world.

* It has 103 elevators and 16,000 windows, and 17,000 people work in the building.

* The floors of each of the nine towers are made of a lighter material than the walls and are suspended between them.

Did you know?

* The tallest skyscraper with brick walls was the Monadnock Building in Chicago. It was built in 1891 and had 16 floors. Its walls were nearly seven feet thick at the bottom!

* The United Nations Building at Lake Success, New York, was one of the first glass-sided skyscrapers to be built.

* Three of the six tallest skyscrapers in the world are in New York City: the World Trade Center (1362 feet, 415 meters), the Empire State Building (1250 feet, 381 meters), and the Chrysler Building (1047 feet, 319 meters).

* The other three of the tallest skyscrapers are all in Chicago: the Sears Tower (1454 feet, 443 meters), the Standard Oil Building (1135 feet, 346 meters) and the John Hancock Center (1129 feet, 344 meters).

Inventions that helped to make skyscrapers possible

1857	Elisha Otis invented a steam operated elevator.
1879	Thomas Edison and Joseph Swan invented electric light.
1887	Otis's company built the first electric elevators.
1932	The PSFS Building in Philadelphia in the United States became one of the first to use air conditioning.

* A skyscraper is being planned to be built in New York City which will be 1834 feet (559 meters) high with 150 stories. This skyscraper, called the Trump City Tower, will be the tallest building in the world.

▶ New York City today.

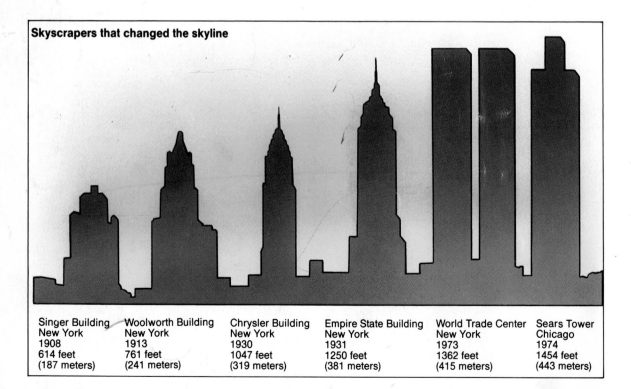

Skyscrapers that changed the skyline

| Singer Building New York 1908 614 feet (187 meters) | Woolworth Building New York 1913 761 feet (241 meters) | Chrysler Building New York 1930 1047 feet (319 meters) | Empire State Building New York 1931 1250 feet (381 meters) | World Trade Center New York 1973 1362 feet (415 meters) | Sears Tower Chicago 1974 1454 feet (443 meters) |

44

The world's highest skyscrapers					
Skyscraper	City	Number of floors	Height in feet/meters	Height compared with its width	Amount of space for offices in acres
Sears Tower	Chicago	110	1454/443	six times its width	99
World Trade Center	New York City	110	1362/415	seven times its width	200
Empire State Building	New York City	102	1250/381	nine times its width	62

Glossary

architect: a person who designs buildings and draws plans for the builders to follow.

bedrock: solid rock below the ground.

borehole: a hole drilled in the ground in order to obtain samples of rock and soil from beneath the surface.

buttress: a structure, usually stone or brick, built up against a wall to add support.

cladding: the layer of building materials used to cover the outside walls of a skyscraper.

compress: to squeeze something into a smaller space by pressure from all sides.

core: the thick column or tube in the center of a skyscraper that makes the whole building strong.

cross braces: strong bars of steel that reach from corner to corner on the side of a building to hold it rigid.

curtain wall: a removable outer wall that does not support any weight.

estimate: the price set on a job before the work is carried out.

formwork: wooden boards used to form the walls of a mold in which concrete is cast.

girder: a long metal beam used for strength and support in large structures such as bridges and skyscrapers.

hull and core: a type of skyscraper with a strong core in the center and a large open space, or hull, between the core and the outer walls.

lift slab: a method of building by preparing concrete floors on the ground and lifting them into position.

load: the strain put upon a building by its own weight.

penthouse: a luxury apartment built on the roof of a building, usually surrounded by a balcony or terrace.

pier: a thick, heavy pillar of steel or concrete used as part of the foundations of a tall building.

pile: a narrow column of steel or concrete driven into solid rock to form part of the foundations of a building.

planning permission: the official approval needed before work on a new building can start.

prefabricated: any part of a building that has been made exactly to size somewhere away from the building site.

pressure sensor: a delicate instrument for measuring changes of air pressure.

pre-stressed concrete: concrete that has been poured over stretched steel rods. The steel rods are unable to shrink back to their original size once the concrete has hardened. This tensioned steel makes the concrete very strong.

raft: a large slab of concrete, making a platform on which a building can be erected and which serves as its foundation.

reinforced concrete: concrete that has been poured over a framework of steel rods and allowed to harden.

rivet: a metal bolt or pin used to join two girders or other structures together.

shell: the frame or skeleton of a building.

shuttering: wooden planks used to mold concrete.

structural engineer: a person who is trained to advise architects on what kind of structure and building materials are best to make a building strong and safe.

tension: the strain felt when things are pulled apart or stretched.

weld: to join metals together by heating them to a high temperature.

wind tunnel: a room where tests are carried out to measure the effects of wind on an object.

Index